# THE
# A-Z
## OF
# HOMEMADE CHUTNEYS, PICKLES & RELISHES

# THE
# A–Z
## OF
# HOMEMADE CHUTNEYS, PICKLES & RELISHES

Words by Amelia Carruthers
Illustrations and Design by Zoë Horn Haywood

# CONTENTS

# CONTENTS

# INTRODUCTION

Welcome to the wonderful world of chutneys, pickles and relishes.

As well as lots of classic recipes, this book is filled with tips and techniques on making the perfect preserve. What's more, you don't even need lots of equipment or a vast array of ingredients to get started. Making your own chutneys, pickles and relishes at home is very often cheaper than buying them - perfect for the thrifty home-chef. The cost of ingredients is low (especially if you grow them yourself), and by creating large batches, you can save a huge amount of money.

It is *incredibly easy* to make chutneys, pickles and relishes at home... Preserving vegetables by turning them into chutney, for example, involves cooking (to reduce the vegetables moisture content and to kill bacteria, yeasts, etc.), flavouring, the addition of vinegar, and sealing within an airtight jar (to prevent recontamination). Thats it! Pickles and relishes are largely similar, but generally involve the addition of vinegar and other spices to often uncooked (or partially cooked) vegetables, producing a slightly 'chunkier' result.

Pickling began 4000 years ago, using cucumbers native to India; the resultant product known as 'achar.' The technique was also used by the Romans, who made a concentrated fish pickle called 'garum.' Although these products arose out of necessity, people enjoyed the resultant flavours too! Chutneys are very similar in preparation and usage to a pickle, and they date back as far as 500 BC. Although also famous as an Indian dish, this method of preserving food actually originated in Northern Europe and was adopted by the British empire, who then started exporting food to the colonies including Australia and America. However, the combination of greater and more varied imports to Britain, as well as new abilities to refrigerate food, meant that chutneys fell out of favour and were relegated to military and colonial use. The British Royal Navy particularly utilised lime pickle/chutney to ward off scurvy on journeys to the new world. Consequently, it was around this time (about 1780) that chutney appeared as a popular appetizer dish in India.

The history of chutneys, pickles and relishes is thus inextricably tied with the history of exploitation and colonisation. British rule over the Indian subcontinent relied on preserved foodstuffs such as lime pickles, chutneys and marmalades. It was only in the nineteenth century that types of chutney such as 'Major Grey's' or 'Bengal Club', specifically created for western tastes, were shipped back to Europe. The tradition of chutney, pickle and relish making then spread quickly through the English-speaking world, especially in the Caribbean and American South, where chutney is still a popular condiment for ham, pork, and fish. Relishes are particularly fashionable in America, with pickled cucumber the most widely available condiment. An especially notable relish is Gentleman's Relish, invented in 1828 by Ben Elvin, which contains spiced Anchovy. It is traditionally spread sparingly atop unsalted butter on toast. Amusingly, Worcester sauce was discovered from a forgotten barrel of special relish in the London basement of the Lea and Perrins Chemist shop!

The marvellous thing about making your own homemade products is the fun one can have with creating customised labels and garnishes to the finished jars (think finely chopped veg, citrus zest, herb sprigs) – a perfect present as well as personal treat. We hope that the reader is inspired by this book to start making their own chutneys, pickles and relishes; a delicious and rewarding pastime.  Enjoy.

**Amelia Carruthers**

# GENERAL
# PRELIMINARIES

Always ensure the fruits or vegetables have been washed thoroughly, especially if they have been gathered from low plants, or trees that are near roads. The recipes in this book will use either 500g or 1kg of vegetables (if this is the main ingredient), which should produce between three and six traditional jam jars, or the equivalent of pickle. These amounts are only a rough guide though, and it is always better to overestimate the amount of jars you many need! The amount of chutney or relish you produce will depend on how strong you wish the end result to be though. Some people prefer much thicker, viscous products, whilst others will only be looking for a 'chunky mix.' Have fun experimenting and just use what you've got!

Within this A-Z, you will find information on how to select your jam jars - as well as how to sterilise and seal them properly. You will also find essential tips what equipment and utensils to buy, information on the all important 'vinegar' and how to select the best and freshest ingredients for your homemade treats. Good luck, and happy cooking.

# RECIPES

# A IS FOR. . . APPLE

Traditional folklore is brimming with references to the apple tree's virtues. This ancient, and thoroughly English tree has provided abundant food for centuries, and has many uses in the kitchen (both sweet and savoury) as well as in herbal remedies. In 1931, when writing Modern Herbal, a Mrs Grieve stated that there used to be 2,000 varieties of apple, but with the unfortunate decline of private orchards, many of these wonderful fruits have been lost. This is a true classic and a great starter recipe, so delicious and so easy to make - perfect with pork and crackling. It would also be wonderful with cold meats or added to a traditional gravy - giving a hint of fruit sweetness to your dishes.

## **Apple Chutney**

### Ingredients

- 1kg cooking apples
- 600g sugar (muscovado or demerara works best)
- 600ml cider vinegar
- 300g raisins
- 2 shallots (regular onions would work just as well)
- 2 tbsps of whole-grain mustard
- 3cm (roughly) of ginger, grated
- A pinch of salt

### Method

1. Core, peel (optional) and roughly chop the apples.

2. Place the apples, along with all the other ingredients into a large, heavy-bottomed saucepan.

3. Bring the temperature up, and cook the ingredients on a medium boil for a couple of minutes.

4. Then, allow to simmer for roughly thirty minutes. Cook until the mixture has obtained a thick, 'jam' like consistency.

5. If sufficiently cooked, remove from the heat and allow to cool slightly.

6. Transfer your warm chutney into warm sterilised jars. Cover with a wax paper disc and seal.

# B IS FOR. . . BEETROOT

Beetroot is a fantastic vegetable; a rich, velvety purple hue, earthy taste and silky smooth texture. It is also incredibly low in fat and packed full of vitamins, minerals and antioxidants. Luckily for us too, it is very easy to grow in the UK - a quintessentially English vegetable. With the advent of World War Two, food shortages and the increased need to preserve food though, pickled beetroot in jars became the most widely available form of this foot stuff. With this in mind, why not hark back to the 'Blitz Spirit' and try this version of Beetroot relish for yourself?

As a 'handy' hint... if your hands become stained whilst preparing the beetroot, just squeeze some lemon juice over them to help remove the purple colour.

# Beetroot Relish

## Ingredients

- 500g Beetroot
- 1 Onion
- 200g sugar
- 250ml white or red
  wine vinegar
- 2 tsps oil

- Pinch of salt
- Spices (to taste):
- Mustard Seeds
- Allspice
- Cinnamon
- 1 Clove

## Method

1. Peel and grate the beetroots.  You should be looking for a small, rough - yet individual texture.

2. Add the mustard seeds to a large heavy-bottomed saucepan on a medium heat. When they start to pop, add the onion (chopped), and then the sugar, oil, vinegar, salt, beetroot and the rest of the spices.

3. Stir everything together to combine - and continue stirring over a medium heat.

4. Once your mixture is combined, leave to cook for at least thirty minutes.  The beetroot should be nice and soft.

5. Add or remove liquid (water will do just fine), as the relish demands.

6. Once your relish is cooked sufficiently, remove from the heat and allow to cool slightly.

7. Place your warm relish into warm, sterilised glass jars.  Cover with a wax paper disc and seal.  Your relish is ready!

# C IS FOR. . CHOW CHOW

Had you heard of 'Chow Chow' before? It is a dish little known in Britain, but highly popular in the United States. It is a relish made from a combination of vegetables, mainly tomato, cabbage, onions, carrots, beans, asparagus, cauliflower and peas. It is traditionally associated with the Southern United States and soul food, as many claim it found its way to the South during the expulsion of the Acadian people from Nova Scotia. Still others cite a connection to the relish recipes of Chinese rail workers in the 1800s and Indian chutneys. Now, its used as a great sweet topping for hot dogs and pinto beans. The vegetables in this recipe are only a suggestion, so do feel free to use whatevers readily available!

## Chow Chow Relish

### Ingredients

- 1 small green cabbage
- 100g onions
- 100g peppers
- 100g cauliflower
- 100g courgette
- 100g carrots
- 400ml vinegar
- 300g sugar
- Spices:
- 2 tbsps wholegrain mustard
- 1 tsp turmeric
- 1 tsp celery seeds
- 2cm ginger (grated)

### Method

1. Combine all the vegetables, either chopped or finely sliced in a large, glass or ceramic bowl with a good sprinkling of salt.

2. Leave the mixture to stand for at least six hours (or overnight). Then, wash the vegetables well under cold water.

3. Place the vinegar, sugar and spices into a large, heavy-bottomed saucepan and cook over a medium heat until all the sugar has dissolved.

4. Then, add all the vegetables and simmer for at least ten minutes. Quickly bring up to the boil, then take it off the heat.

5. Allow the mixture to cool slightly, and then place the warm 'chow chow' into warm, sterilised glass jars. Cover with a wax paper disc and seal. As soon as it cools, it is ready to eat!

# D IS FOR. . . DATES

This wonderfully saccharine, sticky fruit came originally from Iraq, and has been a staple food in the Middle East and the Indus Valley for thousands of years. Dates spread to Europe with the spice trade of the eighteenth century, and have been highly prized ever since. Why not try this unusual ingredient with the addition of rhubarb? Most of the rhubarb grown in England comes from Yorkshire, specifically from the 'Rhubarb Triangle' of Wakefield, Leeds and Bradford, and is recognised as a unique regional food. A true meeting of East and West! The tartness of the rhubarb and the sweetness of the dates work perfectly together in this simple, yet elegant recipe.

## <u>Rhubarb and Date Chutney</u>

### <u>Ingredients</u>

- 500g rhubarb
- 150g dates
- 250g red onions
- 200g apples (standard, eating apples)
- 250g soft, dark sugar

- 200ml wine vinegar
- Spicing to taste (ginger, mustard and curry powder work well)
- A pinch of salt

### <u>Method</u>

1. Finely slice the onions and cook them in a large, heavy-bottomed saucepan with the vinegar, allowing them to simmer for roughly ten minutes.

2. Then, add the rest of the ingredients (spices included) - *except* the rhubarb.

3. Slowly raise the temperature and bring to the boil. Then, lower again and simmer for a further ten minutes until the apples are nice and soft.

4. At this point, add the rhubarb and cook for (roughly) twenty minutes - or until the chutney had gained a thick, 'jam-like' consistency.

5. Take it off the heat, and allow to cool slightly.

6. Place the warm chutney into warm, sterilised jars. Cover with a wax paper disc and seal. If you've got the patience, leave for a month before eating.

# E IS FOR. . . ENDIVE

Endive belongs to the chicory genus, which includes several similar, slightly bitter-tasting leafed vegetables. It is a wonderful vegetable, rich in vitamins and minerals, especially in folate and vitamins A and K, as well as being high in fibre. It also comes in lovely yellow and red colours, and was described in Thomas Jefferson's *Farm Book* as 'one of the greatest acquisitions a farmer can have.' The subtle flavours of thyme and fennel work really well with the delicate endive; providing a distinctive taste to match the slightly bitter undertones. Try this delicious, tangy pickle with sandwiches or summer barbeques!

# Pickled Endive

## Ingredients

- 500g endive
- 100g small, sweet peppers
- 50g sugar
- 2 cloves of garlic
- 300ml vinegar
- 300ml water
- A pinch of:
- cayenne pepper
- thyme
- fennel
- salt

## Method

1. Wash and thickly slice the endive and the peppers.

2. Place the endive and the peppers in a large, ceramic or glass bowl with a generous sprinkling of salt. Mix well.

3. Leave this mixture to infuse for at least four hours. This process will result in a 'crisper' end pickle, as the salt dehydrates them.

4. Once the vegetables have infused with the salt, wash them thoroughly in cold water.

5. Take a large, heavy-bottomed saucepan and add the vinegar, sugar, water, chopped garlic and the spices.

6. Cook on a medium heat - just enough to allow the flavours to combine.

7. Add the endives and peppers to the vinegar solution (once it has cooled) and place in sterilised glass jars. Cover with a wax paper disc and seal.

# F IS FOR. . . FIGS

Native to the Middle East and western Asia, the fig has been sought out and cultivated since ancient times, and is now widely grown throughout the temperate world. Figs have only really been grown in Europe since the sixteenth century though, when Cardinal Reginald Pole introduced fig trees to Lambeth palace in London. Figs were a favourite of wartime Britain, and in the *National Food Campaign Exhibition of 1940,* they were among the fruits recommended for popular consumption. Mixed fruit puddings (containing figs) were especially well-liked, as well as the 'Fig Charlotte' which combined figs, sugar, brown bread and suet - all baked together in a pie-dish and served with custard. Scrumptious. Try this unique sweet pickle with roast meats, or utilise the fig-infused balsamic vinegar for a delicious salad dressing.

## **Pickled Figs in Balsamic Vinegar**

### Ingredients

- 500g figs
- 200g caster sugar
- 225ml balsamic vinegar
- 100ml water

### Method

1. Take a large, heavy-bottomed saucepan and combine the sugar, vinegar and water.

2. Cook over a medium heat until all the sugar has dissolved, and then add the figs (whole).

3. Simmer for roughly ten minutes (or until the figs are just tender).

4. Remove the saucepan from the heat and allow to cool slightly.

5. Place the warm figs into warm, sterilised jars. Cover with a wax paper disc and seal. Your figs should keep for at least six months if properly sealed and refrigerated.

# G IS FOR. . . GHERKIN

The ultimate vegetable of the pickling world! Gherkins are actually a form of savoury pickled cucumber, favoured particularly in Britain and Australia. Like the pickled cucumber, gherkins are great in sandwiches, and are historically associated with Central Europe. Sometimes called a *cornichon* (the French word for gherkin), they have also been known as *horned cucumbers, crumplings* and *guerkins*. Try combining the traditional vinegar and dill flavourings with good sea salt, coriander seeds and garlic. This should provide a wonderfully crisp and fresh result, perfect with rich patés and cheeses.

## **Pickled Gherkins**

### Ingredients

- -1 kg gherkins (small cucumbers)
- -300g salt
- -700ml white vinegar
- -700ml water
- -2 cloves of garlic
- -2 sprigs of dill
- -2 tbsps coriander seeds

### Method

1. Ensure the gherkins are clean and presentable, then gently prick them with a fork.

2. Place the gherkins, along with the salt into a large, ceramic or glass bowl and combine thoroughly.

3. Leave this mixture to infuse for at least four hours. This process will result in a 'crisper' end pickle, as the salt dehydrates them.

4. Once the gherkins have infused with the salt, wash them thoroughly in cold water.

5. Take a large, heavy-bottomed sauce pan and add the vinegar, water, chopped garlic, dill and coriander.

6. Cook very briefly on a low heat - to allow the flavours to combine.

7. Add the gherkins to the vinegar solution, and place in sterilised glass jars. Cover with a wax paper disc and seal.

# H IS FOR. . . HERBS

Here, anything goes! The brilliant thing about making savoury herb chutneys, is that you are in complete control of what you add into them. Once you have mastered the basic technique, you are in charge of the variations. Many herbs make great companions; rosemary and garlic with mint or parsley; fennel and marjoram with lemon thyme; or basil and sage with tarragon. We particularly recommend this version of a classic English apple chutney, flavoured with aromatic but subtle thyme and rosemary. The hint of lemon and garlic ensures a sophisticated finish and it is useful for livening stews, soups and gravies. This combination would be a lovely accompaniment to soft blue cheeses.

## **English Herb Chutney**

### Ingredients

- 500g cooking apples (or pears)
- 150g soft, dark sugar
- 300ml cider vinegar
- 1 sprig of thyme (finely chopped leaves)
- 1 sprig of rosemary (finely chopped leaves)
- 1 lemon (zested)
- 1 clove of garlic

### Method

1.  Core, peel and roughly chop the apples.

2.  Place the apples into a large, heavy-bottomed saucepan. Add the chopped thyme, rosemary, garlic and the lemon zest.

3.  Bring the temperature up, and cook the ingredients on a medium boil for a couple of minutes.

4.  Then, allow to simmer for roughly thirty minutes. Or until the apples (or pears) are nice and soft. The mixture should obtain a thick, 'jam' like consistency.

5.  If sufficiently cooked, remove from the heat and allow to cool slightly.

6.  Transfer your warm herb chutney into warm sterilised jars. Cover with a wax paper disc and seal.

# I IS FOR. . INGREDIENTS

When making chutneys, pickles and relishes, thankfully - there aren't that many staple ingredients. All you will need are vinegar, spices and sugar, possibly salt, herbs or citrus and the 'main ingredient' for your chutney, pickle or relish.

Finding the best ingredients is important though, as the better your initial ingredients are, the better the end-result will be. Look at the local produce on offer in your area. It is so often the case that the best things to eat are the things that grow locally, are in season, and haven't travelled a

huge distance. Not only do these things taste better than their imported counterparts, but it is far kinder to the environment to use what is nearby. Perhaps you have a wonderful local greengrocer who can supply you with seasonal vegetables, or a brilliant local health food shop where you can stock up on herbs and spices? Use your local suppliers and their expertise, as their knowledge will be rather useful to you while you are still getting to grips with the basics.

Making your own chutneys, pickles and relishes is a fantastic way to use up surplus produce. Work out when the vegetables or fruits are in abundance, what time of year is best to pick them, and most importantly, *where* you can find them. In april, the first cabbages might make an appearance, followed in the mid summer months by all range of treats; tomatoes, radishes, onions and nasturtiums... As we move into autumn, delicious veggies such as beetroots and quinces will follow on.  For the more exotic chutney or relish, as well as for necessary ingredients such as lemons or limes, your local food-store should have everything you need.

# J IS FOR. . . JARS

Jam jars are very easy to come across, and should be sold at all local homeware stores as well as larger supermarkets. They come in all sizes and shapes.  You should also try and buy some wax paper tops with which to seal your jars, to prevent air getting in as well as protect the lid from the vinegar. There is really only one technique that you will need to master when it comes to jars though, and that is: Sterilisation.

It is very important that you use sterilised jars to store your chutney, pickle or relish in, both during preparation and in the later stages of the process when you are storing your creations.  This will help them to keep for longer, as it will remove any bacteria, yeasts or fungi and protect your liquids.  Jars and that have not been sterilised properly will infect the food inside, meaning it will spoil very quickly and need to be thrown away. Sterilisation is a very simple process though, and can be done in a number of ways. The simplest way to sterilise your equipment at home is to wash the bottles or jars in very hot soapy water, rinse in more very hot water, and place them into an oven on the lowest setting (275°F/130°C/Gas 1) for twenty minutes.  Ensure you use the bottles when they are still warm, and also that they are airtight when sealed to prevent bacteria entering the bottle.

N.B:  Do not put cold liquids into hot jars, or hot liquids into cold jars; this may result in the glass shattering; a messy and dangerous problem to fix!

# K IS FOR. . . KIMCHI

Kimchi, also spelled kimchee or gimchi, is a traditional fermented Korean side dish made of vegetables and a whole variety of seasonings. It is often described as spicy and sour, and is considered Korea's national dish. It was so popular, that during South Korea's involvement in the Vietnam war, its government requested American help to ensure that South Korean troops, reportedly 'desperate' for the food, could obtain it in the field. There are hundreds of varieties made from napa cabbage, radish, scallion or cucumber as the main ingredient. Early kimchi was made of cabbage and beef stock only though, as red chillies did not come to Korea until the sixteenth century. This recipe is a really simple way to get started on the classic...

## **Cabbage Kimchi**

## Ingredients

- 1 large green cabbage (roughly 900g)
- 200g daikon radish
- 4 medium scallions
- 50g salt (iodene free)
- 5 cloves of garlic
- 3cm piece of ginger
- 1 red chilli
- 1 tsp sugar
- 50ml fish sauce (fresh seafood; crab, anchovies and shrimp heads work well too)

## Method

1. Quarter the cabbage and slice into thick strips. Then, liberally sprinkle the salt over the cabbage, making sure everything is covered.

2. Mix in the salt, combining with your hands until the cabbage has turned limp and slightly watery. Then weigh it down with something heavy, and leave to stand for two hours.

3. Then, rinse the cabbage thoroughly under cold water, to make sure no salty residue remains.

4. Finely grate or chop the garlic, ginger, sugar, chilli and whatever 'fishy flavourings' you wish to add, and place them all in a large bowl. Mix together well to form a light paste.

5. Then, add the drained cabbage along with the radishes to the spice paste - and mix well.

6. Pack your vegetable and spice mix into large jars (kilner clip tops work really well for this, because of the large opening). Weigh the vegetables down with something heavy, until the brine naturally covers them.

7. At this point, you may want to add a little more salt and water solution if there is not enough natural brine.

8. Let the jar stand for up to five days, checking it once a day for the flavour. Make sure the vegetables stay submerged. When the kimchi tastes good to you, it is ready to eat!

# L IS FOR. . . LIME

This recipe really goes to show why home cooking is so rewarding.  Lime pickle can be bought from many stores, and many people would be scared off making it, but this relatively simple pickle is a real treat. It was the saviour of many a sailor on a long voyage, preventing scurvy as well as preventing these precious fruits from going bad.  The British Royal Navy particularly utilised lime pickle to great effect in warding off scurvy on journeys to the new world. Lime pickle is a favourite accompaniment to Indian food, as the juicy, sour limes perfectly compliment the hot spices of a traditional curry.  It can also be served with cold meats, or even better - homemade naan bread, pappadams and samosas to boot. So why not give it a go?

## Lime Pickle

### Ingredients

- 10 limes
- 150g soft brown sugar
- 50ml vegetable oil
- 50ml water
- 50ml vinegar
- 2 tbsps salt

- Spices:
- 2 tsps mustard seeds
- 2 tsps ground cumin
- 2 tsps coriander
- 2 large garlic cloves
- 2cm piece of ginger
- 1 large red chilli

## Method

1. Chop the limes into thick rounds and place them in a large ceramic or glass bowl with the salt. Mix the limes well, making sure that all the fruits are covered in salt.

2. Leave the limes overnight to infuse.

3. Heat the oil in a large, heavy-bottomed saucepan along with the spices. Cook on a medium heat for roughly one minute, until the aromas really come through.

4. Tip in the lime mixture, water, vinegar and sugar and bring everything up to the boil.

5. Then, lower the heat and simmer for at least fifteen minutes, until the mixture has achieved a nice, thick consistency.

6. Take the saucepan off the heat and allow to cool slightly.

7. Pour your warm pickle into warm, sterilised glass jars. Cover with a wax paper disc and seal. Leave the pickle for at least one week, to allow the flavours to really infuse.

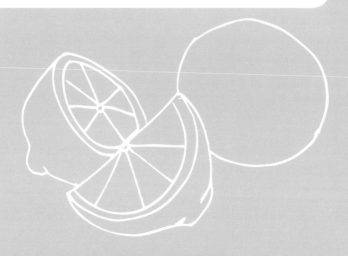

# M IS FOR... MARROW

Marrow is very closely related to courgette, squash and pumpkin - all of which could be used in the same way in a chutney. Its also great to grow yourself, so why not give it a go? Marrow will need a sunny position in well watered soil, preferably away from any cold, windy spots. It should also be sown between april and june, and harvested between july and october. This delicious chutney is a great way to use up surplus produce, and keeps the marrow's subtle flavours at the forefront with the simple addition of onions, apples and just a hint of lemon and ginger. Good luck, and happy growing!

# Marrow Chutney

## Ingredients

- 1kg marrow
- 200g onion
- 200g apples
- 200g demerara or muscovado sugar
- 700ml vinegar
- A good grind of black pepper
- 2cm piece of ginger (sliced)
- 1 lemon (juiced and zested - amount according to taste)

## Method

1. Chop the marrow into small chunks and place in a large ceramic or glass bowl. Sprinkle it with salt, making sure everything is covered, and leave overnight. This will ensure your final chutney is nice and crisp.

2. Once the marrow has been left for at least twelve hours, place it in a large heavy-bottomed saucepan along with the onions (chopped), apples (cored and chopped), ginger, lemon, pepper, sugar and vinegar.

3. Bring everything up to the boil, and then reduce to a simmer. Cook while stirring constantly until the chutney has achieved a lovely thick, 'jam-like' consistency.

4. Once sufficiently cooked, take the saucepan off the heat and allow to cool slightly.

5. Place your warm chutney into warm sterilised glass jars. Cover with a wax paper disc and seal. Your chutney will keep for at least six months if stored in the refrigerator.

# N IS FOR. . . NASTURTIUM

Nasturtiums are also wonderfully easy to grow annual flowers - whose leaves, seeds and flowers are all edible. Their vibrant appearance is the perfect for hanging baskets or plant pots around the front door, whilst their delicate fragrance also is lovely when cut, and placed around the house. These flowers can be grown in slightly shadier spots, but they do not bloom quite so well; sunny, well-drained soil is best. Known as the 'poor man's capers', though a delicacy in their own right, try pickling nasturtium pods, which will appear as the flowers wither away. They have a distinct, mustardy flavour, wonderful with rich meats and blue cheeses.

Tip - do adjust the recipe to as much or as little of these lovely nasturtium pods as you can find.

# Pickled Nasturtium Pods

## Ingredients

- 200g nasturtium pods
- 250ml water
- 200ml white wine vinegar
- 1 tsp sugar
- 1 bay leaf
- 1 sprig of thyme
- 60g salt

## Method

1. Try to harvest the nasturtium pods while they are still young. As they mature, they will lose their crispness and flavour; so check for the bright green, still solid pods.

2. Make sure to rinse the pods, to remove any dirt.

3. Start by dissolving the sugar in the water to make a brine.

4. Place the nasturtium pods in the brine, in a large jar - and leave for a couple of days. This should help the flavours to mellow slightly.

5. After 1-2 days, strain the nasturtium seeds and rinse well in cold water to remove any excess salt.

6. Place the vinegar and sugar in a large, heavy-bottomed saucepan and stir until the sugar has completely dissolved. At this point, add some finely chopped thyme leaves.

7. Place the nasturtium seeds into the jam jars you are going to use, and pour over the still hot-vinegar and sugar solution. Add a bay-leaf too.

8. Wait for the mixture to cool slightly, then cover with a wax paper disc and seal. Your nasturtium pods are ready to eat - though the flavours will mature with time.

# O IS FOR... ONION

The ultimate classic pickle! Onions are a really fun vegetable to grow at home; making a spectacular transformation from seed - to spindly grass, to round and ripe vegetable. They are also an incredibly versatile foodstuff, featured in so many recipes, both savoury and sweet. Onions only need a little water, but good, sunny and well-weeded soil is crucial. Plant your onions outside in March or April, and harvest your well-earned vegetables from july to september. This is a true traditional English recipe, a national treasure which is simple as well as delicious. Try with British classics such as fish and chips, ploughmans lunch or pork pies.

# Pickled Onions

## Ingredients

- 1 kg white, small onions
- 200g sugar (or double the amount of honey)
- 1 litre malt vinegar
- 20g salt
- Spices: Coriander, mustard seeds, black peppercorns and chili flakes (to taste)

## Method

1. Peel your onions (this will involve a lot of eye-watering, but placing a spoon in your mouth supposedly helps!)

2. Sprinkle the salt generously over the onions, and leave overnight in a large, ceramic or glass bowl. This will help your onions stay nice and crisp in the final pickle.

3. Place the sugar (or honey), spices and vinegar into a large, heavy-bottomed saucepan. Cook voer a medium heat, stirring the sugar until it has completely dissolved.

4. Pack the onions into the jam jars you wish to use, and pour over the still hot vinegar syrup. Make sure each jar has the same amount of pickling spices, and the liquid completely covers the onions.

5. Cover with a wax paper disc and seal. Your pickled onions should be left for at least one month before consuming, as this will give the flavours time to mellow. Enjoy.

# P IS FOR... PICCALILLI

Piccalilli is an English interpretation of a classic Indian pickle; a relish of chopped pickled vegetables (most usually cauliflower and marrow) and spices. The *Oxford English Dictionary* traces the word to the middle of the eighteenth century when, in 1758, Hannah Glasse described how 'to make Paco-Lilla, or Indian Pickle.' Our modern recipes, and the one listed here - are all derivations from this original dish. Today, piccalilli is produced both commercially and domestically, the latter product being a mainstay of Women's Institute and farmhouse stalls; delicious as well as cheap to produce. A perfect start for the home-relisher! Here, personal adaptations and experimentation is key, so use whatever vegetables you have to hand...

# Classic Piccalilli Relish

## Ingredients

- 1kg Vegetables (of roughly equal amounts). Try…
-Cauliflower Florets
-Cucumber
-French Beans
-Garden Marrow
-Pickled Onions (see above!)
-Spices:
-1 tblsp whole-grain mustard

-1 tsp ginger (ground or more grated)
-1 tsp turmeric
-1 large clove of garlic
-500ml white malt vinegar
-100g sugar (again, demerara or muscovado work best)
-2 ttblsp cornflour
-Salt (to taste)

## Method

1. Place the vegetables and salt in a glass or ceramic bowl. Leaving the vegetables and the salt overnight will result in crisper pickles, as the salt helps to pull the moisture out of the vegetables and makes them crisper.

2. The next morning, discard the liquid, rinse and dry the vegetables.

3. Place the vinegar and spices into a large, heavy-bottomed saucepan and bring to the boil.

4. Add the vegetables to the vinegar and bring down to a simmer. Cook on a very low temperature for about twenty minutes, or until the vegetables are tender.

5. Add the sugar and cornflour to the mix, stirring constantly. It should start to thicken.

6. If sufficiently cooked, remove the piccalilli from the heat and allow to cool slightly.

7. Put the warm mix into warm, sterilised jars. Cover with a wax paper disc and seal. Store for at least three weeks before opening!

# Q IS FOR. . . QUINCE

Quince Charming: Quince are small fruits which belong to the same family as pears - and a much under-used and under-appreciated British fruit. Quince trees were first recorded in Britain in 1275, when Edward I planted four at the Tower of London. They may have arrived earlier though, as thirteenth century English recipes included pie-crusts filled with whole quinces coated in honey and sprinkled with ginger. They are grown all over England, and are a treat to find. Pick them in October or November, leaving to ripen in a cool place if necessary. Quince trees are often propagated for their pretty pink flowers, but can also be used for a wonderfully light chutney. Quince has an earthy flavour, almost a cross between an apple and a pear, and is commonly used as an accompaniment to cheese...

## Quince Chutney

### Ingredients

- 500g quinces
- 500g apples
- 500ml vinegar
- 1 large red onion
- 400g muscovado or demerara sugar
- Spices (optional, to taste) - ginger, cumin, mixed spice, cayenne pepper
- A pinch of salt

### Method

1. Core, chop and peel the quinces and the apples. Slice the onion.

2. Place the fruits and vegetables in a large saucepan, along with half the vinegar and cook over a medium heat.

3. Cook the until the fruit is just soft. Then, add the sugar, spices and a pinch of salt.

4. Simmer all the ingredients together until a thick, 'jam-like' consistency has been achieved. This should take roughly twenty minutes.

5. Take the saucepan off the heat, and allow to cool slightly.

6. Pour your warm quince chutney into warm, sterilised glass jars. Cover with a wax paper disc and seal. Voila, your chutney is ready to eat!

# R IS FOR... RADISH

Radishes are a very easy vegetable to grow; full of nutrients and great for the British climate. Their roots should be ready to harvest within four weeks of sowing them, fantastic if you are growing with children. Like onions, ensure that the soil in which your radishes are placed is well-weeded as well as watered. Their green tops are also edible and will make a delicious pesto when diced with parmesan, oil and pine-nuts. Perfect on a summer pasta dish. You can sow your radishes constantly between march and september to ensure an almost year-round supply. This relish has a wonderful pink tone, with a slightly spicy taste - it would make a great summer time accompaniment to barbecued meats.

# Radish Relish

## Ingredients

- 500g radishes (stemmed)
- 1 red onion
- 20g salt
- 200ml vinegar
- 200g sugar
- 1 tbsp wholegrain mustard
- 1 tbsp horseradish

## Method

1. Finely chop (or slice) the radishes and onions.

2. Leave the radishes and onions in a large, glass or ceramic bowl for at least a few hours, to ensure your end relish is nice and crisp.

3. Strain the radish and onion, and wash thoroughly in cold water.

4. Place everything in a large, heavy-bottomed saucepan (including the vinegar, sugar, mustard and horseradish).

5. Bring it up to a gentle boil and cook for about fifteen minutes, or until everything is slightly softened.

6. When sufficiently cooked, take the saucepan off the heat and allow to cool slightly.

7. Pour your warm radish relish into warm, sterilised jars. Cover with a wax paper disc and seal. Your radish is ready to eat.

# S IS FOR. . . SAUERKRAUT

Sauerkraut, directly translated as 'sour cabbage' is finely cut cabbage that has been fermented. This gives it a longer shelf-life and a distinctive sour flavour, wonderful as a condiment on various meats and sandwiches. Although famed as a traditional German dish, pickled cabbage is mentioned by the Roman writer Cato (in his *De Agri Cultura*) and Columella (in his *De re Rustica*). Such dishes also provided much needed nutrients to the British population in times of hardship, especially during winter. In fact, the British explorer James Cook always took a store of sauerkraut on his sea voyages, since experience had taught him it prevented scurvy. If it was good enough for an intrepid explorer, its good enough for us!

## Sauerkraut

### Ingredients

- 1 green cabbage (red cabbage will work too)
- 1 ½ tbsps salt
- 1 tbsp caraway seeds (optional flavouring)

### Method

1. Sauerkraut needs so few ingredients, because when combined with the salt, the cabbage releases its own juices, forming a natural brine.

2. Discard the outer leaves of the cabbage, and very finely slice the rest of it (avoiding the core).

3. Transfer the cabbage, with the salt to a large glass or ceramic bowl, and mix in the salt, combining with your hands until it has turned limp and slightly watery.

4. Pack the cabbage into jars (larger kilner clip tops work best). Make sure to pour any remaining liquid over the cabbage in the jar.

5. Weigh the cabbage down with something flat and heavy, then cover the jar with some cloth and rubber bands. If it needs extra liquid to keep it fully submerged, add a little salt and water solution.

6. Place the jar in a cool, dark place and allow it to ferment for about ten days. Taste as you go though, and if it tastes good, seal the jar and place in the refrigerator.

7. How long the sauerkraut ferments for is completely up to you, it should keep for at least four months when sealed and refrigerated though.

# T IS FOR. . . TOMATO

Tomatoes were not grown in England until the 1590s, and people used to believe they were poisonous! In fact the raw fruit does have low levels of tomatine (found in the stalks) but is not dangerous. Consequently, tomatoes were not widely eaten before the early eighteenth century, but were soon consumed in Britain as soups, broths and as a garnish. This classic chutney is very simple to make, and perfect with a thick slice of English cheddar and bread, or even with a burger or vegetable curry. It is versatile and not too sweet, perfect for preserving a summer glut of this lovely vegetable. A juicy and spicy concoction, unripe green tomatoes can even be used too - great for using up a great little fruit which would otherwise go to waste!

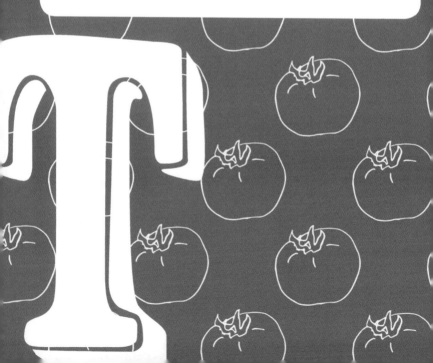

# Tomato Chutney

## Ingredients

- 1kg tomatoes
- 500g red onions
- Spices:
- 3 large garlic cloves
- 1 small chilli
- 3cm ginger
- ½ tbsp paprika
- 250g sugar (demerara or muscovado)
- 150ml wine vinegar

## Method

1. Chop the tomatoes, chilli, garlic and ginger, and finely slice the onions.

2. Place all the ingredients into a large, heavy-bottomed saucepan.

3. Bring the temperature up, and cook the ingredients on a medium boil for a couple of minutes.

4. Then, allow to simmer for roughly forty-five minutes. Cook until the mixture has obtained a thick, 'jam' like consistency.

5. If sufficiently cooked, remove from the heat and allow to cool slightly.

6. Transfer your warm chutney into warm sterilised jars. Cover with a wax paper disc and seal.

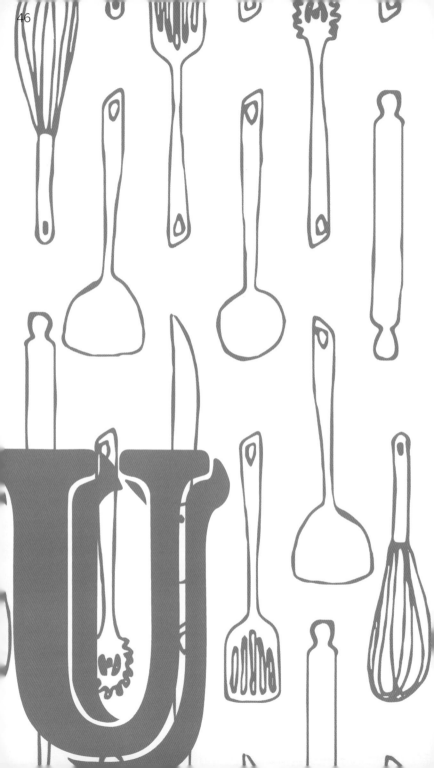

# U IS FOR. . . UTENSILS

Thankfully, for small-scale home cooking, you will need very little specialist equipment. The list of utensils and equipment is not huge, but it is important you have the basics at your fingertips. Your kitchen utensils are the tools of your trade, as it were, and you'll get the best results from your chutney, pickle or relish making if you take the time to source the right ones.

You will need saucepans (heavy-bottomed jam boilers work best), any earthenware or non-porous bowls and plenty of glass jars (for storage; size and amount dependent on the batch size you are intending), as well as occasionally a sieve for straining. Wax paper discs to seal the jars will protect the lids against the vinegars acidic properties. Sharp knives are also invaluable, and will save you a lot of time and effort! Wooden spoons are great for stirring at high temperatures (as they do not conduct heat), and metal spoons are better for skimming off any unwanted pieces which may rise to the surface.

## Check List:

- Saucepan (preferably heavy-bottomed)
- Bowls (for storing the fruit or vegetables)
- Large Spoons (wooden are the most useful)
- Sharp Knives (for finely chopping the vegetables!)
- Glass Jars (for storage and presentation)
- Waxed Discs (to protect your jam jars' lids)

# V IS FOR. . . VINEGAR

Vinegar is used in all the chutney, pickle and relish recipes listed in this book, so it is worthwhile getting to know this important ingredient! Vinegar is a liquid consisting mainly of 'acetic acid' and water. The acid is produced by the fermentation of ethanol by acetic acid bacteria. Today, vinegar is mainly used as a cooking ingredient, but historically, as the most easily available mild acid, it had a great variety of industrial, medicinal and domestic uses.

There are so many different types of vinegar, including apple cider, balsamic, date, honey, malt, rice, sherry, wine, distilled white versions… the list goes on.  It was first discovered in ancient civilisations when grape juice was accidentally left - and turned into wine.  Wine in turn, if also left undisturbed, turned into vinegar.  Whilst this was not such a welcome transformation, over time, the multitudinous uses of vinegar were discovered.  Helen of Troy apparently bathed in vinegar to relax, whilst Cleopatra demonstrated its powers of solvency by dissolving pearls in the liquid to win a  bet that she could consume a fortune.

Today, vinegar is commonly used in food preparation, in particular the pickling processes, vinaigrettes and other salad dressings.  It is also an ingredient in sauces such as mustard, ketchup and mayonnaise.  It is also, as we have already discovered, used when making chutneys and other condiments.  Its preservative qualities mean that vinegar can last indefinitely without the use of refrigeration - a truly useful foodstuff!

# W IS FOR. . . WALNUT

Walnut relishes are very popular in France, but a relative rarity in England. This is a shame, because it really is a fantastic preserve which allows one to enjoy this nutrient-rich nut in a variety of ways. It is an ancient foodstuff which originated in Persia, but is now known as the 'English walnut.' Try if you can to retain the texture of the walnuts, by not making your relish too fine and avoid over-indulging on the sugar. Less is more in this recipe. The bright peppers will also add a bit of excitement and spice to the relish; and you can experiment with a couple of spicy / sweet red peppers too. It will be delicious with really simple dishes; meats, eggs and pulses - as its sweet earthy nature will allow the more subtle flavours to sing.

## **Red Pepper and Walnut Relish**

### Ingredients

- 100g walnuts
- 500g red peppers
- 100ml balsamic vinegar
- 50g sugar
- 1 clove garlic
- 1 tbsp olive oil
- 1 tsp harissa (paprika would work just as well)
- 1 tsp lemon juice
- A pinch of salt

### Method

1. Lightly toast the walnuts in the oven, until they have slightly darkened in colour (this should take roughly ten minutes).

2. Lightly roast the peppers, until they have softened sufficiently (this will probably take about twenty minutes).

3. Once cool, coarsely chop the walnuts and seed, top and chop the peppers.

4. Combine the peppers with the garlic, oil, salt, harissa, lemon juice and sugar - mix well, and then add the walnuts.

5. Your simple relish is ready to be decanted! Just place the warm mixture into warm, sterilised jars. Cover with a wax paper disc and seal. It is best left for three days before serving, to allow the flavours to properly combine.

# X IS FOR... XMAS!

This is a lovely festive recipe, which uses the rich, ruby-red fruit; cranberries - spiced with a hint of cinnamon. Most widely used and grown in North America, cranberries are a fantastic little berry, rich in vitamins C, D, potassium and iron. They are also believed to be a natural remedy for a whole host of health conditions. Cranberries really do come into their own around Christmas, and no hostess's cupboard would be complete without some homemade cranberry relish. They are good for much more than merely accompanying the turkey though, and you can use this citrus-hinted relish in both sweet and savoury dishes. As cranberries can be quite tart and sour, especially when under ripe, do feel free to add more sugar to according to taste.

## **Cranberry and Orange Relish**

Ingredients

- 500g cranberries
- 1 orange (juiced and zested)
- 2cm piece of ginger
- 100g muscovado sugar
- 1 cinnamon stick
- A good splash of port (optional!)

Method

1. Place the cranberries in a large, heavy-bottomed saucepan and cook them on a low heat until nice and soft.

2. Peel the orange, and slice it very finely. Then juice it too, and add this peel and the juice to the cranberries, followed by the ginger (finely grated), sugar and the cinnamon stick.

3. Cook everything on a medium heat for about five minutes to allow the flavours to combine.

4. When the mixture has thickened slightly, pour in the port to loosen it up (here, water would work just as well). Stir in.

5. Pour your orange and cranberry relish into warm, sterilised jars. Cover with a wax paper disc and seal. Your relish is ready to eat!

# Y IS FOR. . . YULETIDE

Chilli Chutney is another fantastic addition to the traditional festive feast. The Chili Pepper gets is spicy flavour from a substance called capsaicin, and vastly varies from the relatively mild cayenne pepper to the scorching habanero; known for its unique combination of intense flavour, aroma and heat.  Upon their introduction into Europe, chilis were grown as botanical curiosities in the gardens of Spanish and Portuguese monasteries. But monks experimented with the chili's culinary potential and discovered that their pungency offered a substitute for black peppercorns, which at the time were so costly that they were used as legal currency in some countries. They are relatively easy to grow at home though, even in the mild English climate, so why not give them a go?  Feel free to make this recipe as spicy or as mild as you like, according to personal preference.

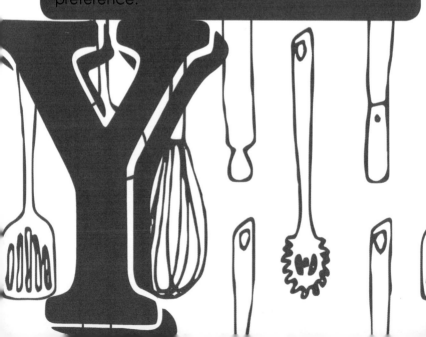

## Chilli Chutney

### Ingredients

- 500g tomatoes
- 200g apples
- 2 large red onions
- 2-3 red chillies (according to taste)
- 100g sugar
- 200ml white wine vinegar
- 1 tbsp tomato purée
- 1 tbsp paprika
- 1 tbsp olive oil

### Method

1. Place the onions (finely chopped) alongside a splash of oil in a large, heavy-bottomed saucepan.

2. Cook them over a medium heat until slightly translucent (for about ten minutes).

3. Then, add the tomatoes, apples, tomato puree, paprika and chilli. Cook for a further five minutes at least – or until everything has started to break down.

4. Stir in the sugar and vinegar, making sure to stir regularly until the sugar has dissolved.

5. Bring the heat down to a low simmer, and cook until it has achieved a thick, 'jam-like' consistency.

6. Allow the mixture to cool slightly. Pour it into warm, sterilised glass jars. Cover with a wax paper disc and seal. Your chutney is ready to eat!

# Z IS FOR. . . ZEST

Citrus fruits make wonderful-tasting tangy chutneys and pickles, and this one will have the most gorgeous, vibrant colour thanks to the lemon's natural hue. The first substantial cultivation of lemons in Europe began in Genoa in the middle of the fifteenth century. The lemon was later introduced to the Americas and beyond in 1493 when Christopher Columbus brought them along on his voyages. This recipe for spiced lemon chutney is a classic recipe to master; and will accompany such a wide variety of dishes; think middle eastern meats and couscous concoctions. This recipe uses the juice, rinds and zest- really making the most of this wonderful fruit.

## **<u>Roasted Lemon Chutney</u>**

<u>Ingredients</u>

- 500g Lemons (unwaxed)
- 2 shallots
- Spices (optional):
- 1 red chilli
- 1 clove of garlic

- 2cm piece of ginger (grated)
- ½ tsp coriander seeds
- A pinch of salt
- Olive oil (for roasting the lemons)

<u>Method</u>

1. Cut the lemons into roughly centimetre wide circles and remove the seeds. Place them on a baking tray with a small drizzle of olive oil and a little salt over the top.

2. Finely chop the shallots, drizzle with the oil and a little salt and place on a separate baking tray.

3. Roast both the lemons and the shallots - they will probably need about twenty minutes, or just until they start to brown.

4. Once everything is cooked, place the lemons, shallots and spices (if you wish) in a large, heavy-bottomed sauce pan and mash with a fork. Although not quite *How They Used To Do It,* a food processor would speed up the process!

5. Bring the mixture to a gentle simmer, and cook just for a few minutes to ensure all the flavours are combined.

6. Place the warm chutney into warm, sterilised jars. Cover with a wax paper disc and seal. Leave for at least a week before opening.

# SERVING S

There are so many ways to serve pickles, chutneys and relishes, and hopefully we have given you some ideas with each recipe. The great thing about them, is that they can be paired with savoury or sweet foods alike - think quince or apple with cheese or rabbit, piccalilli with cold meats, cranberry with stuffing, date chutney with chocolate desserts or figs with ice cream. The list goes on. Try to think of the fruit, vegetable or flavouring on its own, and what foods you would pair that with normally – and then exactly the same will apply to your chutney, pickle or relish! For the beginners, try experimenting by using a new flavour in a tried and tested recipe. Half the fun is in the trialling, so be brave...

As we've already noted, the wonderful thing about making your own homemade products is the fun one can have with creating customised labels and garnishes to the finished jars (think berries, citrus zest, herb sprigs). For the fruity chutneys, a few of the actual ingredients or even some of their flowers are beautiful accompaniments. Exactly the same

# GGESTIONS

applies for the vegetables, herbs and spices; whatever main ingredient you have used, save some back for decoration afterwards. Pickles, chutneys and relishes really do make the perfect present as well as personal treat.

Make sure to source some lovely glass jars (kilner 'clip tops' work well, as do the traditional jam jar which you will find in most homeware stores). This will instantly make your creations look the part. As well as this, for serving chutneys or relishes at dinner parties, there are so many wonderfully decorated plates and bowls, so have a bit of fun! At this point, you can make your own tags (think brown card and twine) to hang around the top of the jars, as well as handwritten labels to adorn the your containers. You could also place a little square of material ('gingham' is always lovely, though 'paisley' would also look a treat) over the top of your jar. Tied with some twine, this gives a great vintage-inspired twist to your presents, and we're sure the recipients will be touched by your efforts. Good luck, and happy decorating.

# TEN TOP TIP

1. The vegetables should *always* be sound, preferably slightly under-ripe – clean and dry. Produce picked in wet (or even continuously foggy weather) makes chutneys and relishes which will develop mould in a very short time.

2. Use the natural seasons as your inspiration for ingredients - this is a great way to explore. Experiment with the recipes in this book, and just use what is growing, cheap and accessible near to you.

3. Always stir well (when cooking is required) to prevent sticking. A slightly undercooked chutney is preferable to one which tastes ever so slightly burnt.

4. Do not use *too* large quantities of fruit or vegetables at a time – large quantities are extremely difficult to handle without the proper equipment.

5. Always have warm, sterilised jars ready for your chutneys, pickles and relishes. Sterilisation is really easy. The simplest way is to wash the jars in very hot soapy water, rinse in more very hot water, and place them into an oven on the lowest setting (275°F/130°C/Gas 1) for twenty minutes.

# AND TRICKS

6. A pinch of bicarbonate of soda, added to very tart fruits (such as lemon or lime pickle) counteracts the acid, and less sugar is required.

7. Whole spices are generally better than the ground spices, as they retain their strength longer. Use them whole if you can in pickles. If ground spice is used (for instance, in a chutney), freshly ground is best.

8. The type of vinegar you use is important: distilled white vinegar will not colour your ingredients, whilst cider vinegar gives a richer, slightly mellower flavour. Malt vinegar in turn, will provide a delicate, almost sweet taste.

9. Cover with cold spiced vinegar for a crisp pickle (red or white cabbage), use boiling vinegar for a soft pickle (beetroot).

10. Store in a cool, dry place. The greatest enemies to chutneys, pickles and relishes are mould and discoloration. As long as they do not encounter any steam or heat after production, and relatively little light, your products should keep for a very long time.

## BUT MOST IMPORTANTLY, JUST HAVE FUN!

Two Magpies

Copyright © 2013 Two Magpies Publishing

An imprint of Read Publishing Ltd
Home Farm, 44 Evesham Road, Cookhill, Alcester,
Warwickshire, B49 5LJ

Commissioning Editor Rose Hewlett
Words by Amelia Carruthers
Design and Illustrations by Zoë Horn Haywood

British Library Cataloguing-in-Publication Data A
catalogue record for this book is available from
the British Library.

Printed in Great Britain
by Amazon